HOW IS PAPER MADE?

DISCARD

By Demi Jackson

Gareth Stevens
PUBLISHING

D0907444

Please visit our website, www.garethstevens.com. For a free color catalog of all our high-quality books, call toll free 1-800-542-2595 or fax 1-877-542-2596.

Library of Congress Cataloging-in-Publication Data

Jackson, Demi, author.
 How is paper made? / Demi Jackson.
    pages cm. — (Everyday mysteries)
 Includes bibliographical references and index.
 ISBN 978-1-4824-3821-5 (pbk.)
 ISBN 978-1-4824-3822-2 (6 pack)
 ISBN 978-1-4824-3823-9 (library binding)
 1. Paper—Juvenile literature. 2. Papermaking—Juvenile literature. I. Title. II. Series:
Everyday mysteries.
 TS1105.5.J33 2016
 676—dc23

                                    2015021552

Published in 2016 by
Gareth Stevens Publishing
111 East 14th Street, Suite 349
New York, NY 10003

Copyright © 2016 Gareth Stevens Publishing

Designer: Katelyn E. Reynolds
Editor: Kristen Nelson

Photo credits: Cover, p. 1 JTB Photo/UIG via Getty Images; pp. 3–24 (background) Natutik/Shutterstock.com; p. 5 Universal History Archive/UIG via Getty Images; p. 7 Brian Balster/Shutterstock.com; p. 9 portumen/Shutterstock.com; p. 11 Moreno Soppelsa/Shutterstock.com; p. 13 Oliver Bunic/Bloomberg via Getty Images; p. 15 safakcakir/Shutterstock.com; p. 17 bikeriderlondon/Shutterstock.com; p. 19 marcovarro/Shutterstock.com; p. 21 Dorling Kindersley/Getty Images.

Printed in the United States of America

CPSIA compliance information: Batch #CW16GS: For further information contact Gareth Stevens, New York, New York at 1-800-542-2595.

CONTENTS

Boldface words appear in the glossary.

An Old Process

People have been making paper for about 2,000 years! Even after all that time, the **process** has stayed very much the same. The biggest difference is the use of machines in papermaking today.

A. Freschi sculpsit

Start in the Forest

Very often, papermaking begins with trees. Sometimes the trees are grown specially to be made into paper. On tree farms, trees are cut down for papermaking, and new trees are planted in their place.

At the Paper Mill

After they're cut down, the trees are taken to a paper mill. They're cleaned, and their **bark** is removed. The wood is chopped into small pieces. Now, it needs to be turned into **pulp**.

paper mill

Wood becomes pulp in two ways, depending on the kind of paper being made. For weaker paper, a machine **grinds** the wood into pulp. For stronger paper, the wood pieces are added to a mix of water and **chemicals**.

pulp

11

Remove the Water

The pulp is cleaned and sometimes dyed a color. At this time, the pulp is mostly water! Machines spread it onto **screens**. Water drips through the screens, and the wood **fibers** start to bind together. This starts to look like a thin mat.

Still more water needs to be removed! The wood pulp mat is fed into huge machines with hot rolling parts. These press out the remaining water and create rolls of paper up to 30 feet (9.1 m) wide!

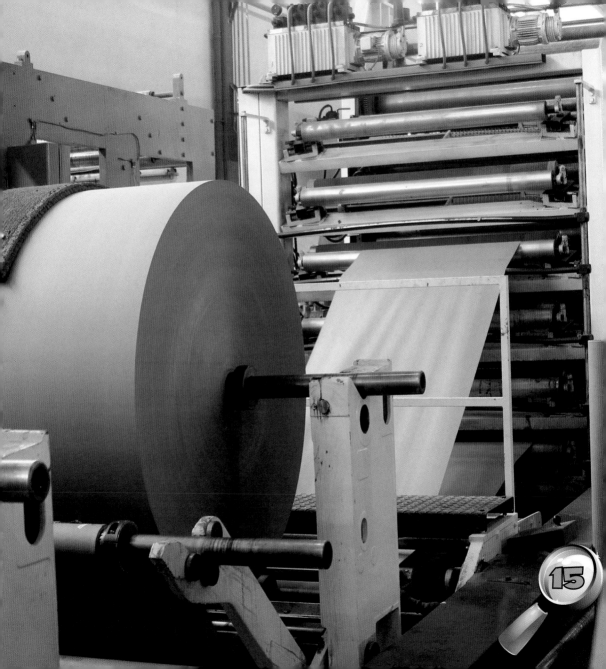

Recycle Your Paper

The big rolls of paper made in a paper mill are cut into sizes people can use. But what happens when we're done with paper? We should recycle it! Recycling is the process of making something new from something used.

recycle

17

New paper can be made from the paper you recycle! Used paper is cut into little pieces and mixed with water. This pulp is cleaned, and water is removed in much the same way it is when making paper from wood.

FOR MORE INFORMATION

BOOKS

Hansen, Amy S. *What Is It Made Of?* Vero Beach, FL: Rourke Publishing, 2012.

Herrington, Lisa M. *Trees to Paper.* New York, NY: Children's Press, 2013.

WEBSITES

How Wood Is Processed!
woodmagic.vt.edu/kids/Products/paper1.htm
Read about how paper is made, and try an activity to make it yourself!

Paper Facts—Kids Go Green
your.caerphilly.gov.uk/kidsgogreen/fact-zone/paper-facts
Find out how paper is recycled.

INDEX